INSPIRED BY DR. MEGAN ANNA NEFF

The
Autistic
Burnout
Cookbook

Nourishing recovery with soothing meals,
safe foods, and sensory-friendly support,

**BONUS
28 Days
Meal plan**

Table of contents

Introduction

Feeding Yourself When the World Is Too Much

Autistic burnout is not simply exhaustion. It is the unraveling of one's inner world—a deep depletion of emotional, cognitive, and physical resources brought on by sustained masking, sensory overload, and relentless social expectations. During these periods, even the most basic acts of self-care—like eating—can feel impossible. Decision fatigue, texture sensitivity, and executive dysfunction all collide to make food an overwhelming obstacle instead of a source of comfort.

This cookbook was born out of that reality.

The Autistic Burnout Cookbook is not about culinary perfection, gourmet artistry, or dietary fads. It is about survival. It is about nourishment without shame. It is about reclaiming the act of feeding yourself—on your terms.

Inside, you will not find complicated meal plans or elaborate techniques. You will find gentle, sensory-considerate recipes. You will find soft foods for shutdowns and crunchy snacks that soothe. You will find meals that can be made with five ingredients, or even no cooking at all. You will find validation. You will find support.

This is a guide for when you can't peel yourself off the floor. For when your fridge feels like a puzzle and your body feels like static. For when the world expects you to "just eat something," but your brain and body say otherwise.

Food is not the cure for burnout—but it *is* a foundation for recovery. And you deserve to eat in ways that honor your needs, not punish your difference.

You are not lazy. You are not broken. You are burned out—and you are still worthy of care.

Let this book be your gentle companion through the fog.

What is Autistic Burnout?

Autistic burnout is a state of intense physical, mental, and emotional exhaustion uniquely experienced by autistic individuals. It is different from typical stress or tiredness.. Instead, it is a prolonged and often debilitating collapse of functioning that can occur after extended periods of masking, overstimulation, social demands, and unmet needs. While many people experience stress, autistic burnout cuts deeper—it impacts identity, executive functioning, sensory processing, and the ability to communicate or perform even routine tasks.

Symptoms of Autistic Burnout may include:

Extreme fatigue or physical weakness

Loss of previously acquired skills

Increased sensitivity to sensory input

Difficulty with speech, communication, or emotional expression

Reduced ability to handle everyday tasks (e.g., cooking, hygiene)

Heightened anxiety, depression, or emotional numbness

Increased need for solitude and downtime

Feeling disconnected from self or identity

Autistic burnout is often misunderstood—even within medical or psychological communities—because it doesn't align with typical definitions of burnout seen in neurotypical populations. For many autistic people, burnout is not a temporary slump; it can last for months or even years, with long-term impacts on independence, self-esteem, and overall health.

It often arises after long periods of "masking," or suppressing autistic traits to fit into non-autistic social norms. Whether it's forcing eye contact, engaging in exhausting conversations, or enduring sensory discomfort in public spaces, this constant self-suppression takes a massive toll over time.

Common triggers of autistic burnout include:

Chronic sensory overload (e.g., noisy workplaces, harsh lighting)

High social demands and frequent masking

Unmet support needs or lack of accommodations

Life transitions or unexpected changes in routine

Ongoing emotional labor and people-pleasing

Suppressed meltdowns, shutdowns, or stimming needs

Burnout is not a sign of weakness. It is a signal that your nervous system has been operating beyond capacity. Autistic burnout is a valid and painful experience, and it requires not just rest—but compassionate, tailored recovery strategies.

The Role of Food in Recovery

When autistic burnout strikes, eating can become overwhelming or even impossible. The sensory world of food—its textures, smells, sounds, and temperatures—can suddenly feel unbearable. Executive dysfunction may make it hard to plan a meal, follow a recipe, or even remember how to boil water. Appetite may fluctuate wildly: some people lose all interest in eating, while others crave familiar or "safe" foods with comforting textures and flavors.

Food, however, is fundamental to healing.

Eating isn't just about fueling the body—it's about regulating the nervous system, stabilizing blood sugar, and restoring energy to a brain that's been running on fumes. In times of burnout, the *how* of eating is just as important as the *what*. That means making food that meets you where you are—not where others think you "should" be.

Why Food Matters During Burnout

Nutritional Support for the Brain
In times of burnout, the brain requires more energy and nutrients to function properly. B vitamins, magnesium, omega-3 fatty acids, and amino acids all play essential roles in mood regulation, cognitive clarity, and nervous system function. Simple, nourishing meals—even when minimal—can help replenish what burnout depletes.

Stabilizing Blood Sugar and Mood
Skipping meals or relying solely on sugary snacks can lead to blood sugar crashes that intensify irritability, fatigue, and anxiety. Including steady, slow-burning carbohydrates, proteins, and healthy fats helps maintain a more

stable internal rhythm—critical when everything feels chaotic.

Reconnecting With the Body

Autistic burnout can create dissociation or a sense of disconnect from bodily cues like hunger, fullness, or thirst. Gentle eating routines help rebuild trust with your body, bringing awareness back without judgment or pressure.

Comfort, Ritual, and Control

Familiar foods with safe textures and predictable tastes can provide a sense of grounding. Having repetitive meals or "food routines" isn't a weakness—it's a form of self-comfort and regulation. Having meals you can return to again and again offers a feeling of structure when the world feels unpredictable.

Minimizing Decision Fatigue

One of the most exhausting parts of eating while burned out is *deciding what to eat*. That's why this cookbook offers not just recipes, but also pre-assembled meal kits, visual instructions, and minimal-ingredient options. These tools are designed to remove friction and lower the mental load.

How to Use This Cookbook

This cookbook is not like others. It is not here to impress or overwhelm you with fancy plating or complicated steps. It is here to support you—gently, consistently, and without judgment—whether you're barely managing to eat or slowly finding your way back to the kitchen.

You can use this book in whatever way works best for you. Take what you need, leave what you don't, and trust your own pace.

Core Features of This Cookbook

Sensory-Friendly Recipes

All recipes in this book consider texture, flavor intensity, temperature, and ease of digestion. You'll find meals categorized by sensory profile: soft foods for shutdowns, crunchy foods for oral stimulation, neutral-flavored dishes for hypersensitive days, and temperature-adjusted options for thermally sensitive eaters.

Low-Spoon Cooking Options

Some recipes are tagged with "low-spoon" indicators—meaning they require minimal effort, no chopping, or can be made entirely in a microwave or toaster oven. These are ideal for days when executive dysfunction is high and energy is low.

Visual Recipe Guides

Select recipes come with visual instructions to reduce the need for text processing. These are especially helpful during shutdowns or for individuals who are non-speaking or have limited reading capacity while burned out.

Meal Kits & Batch Options

You'll find meal kits with simple combinations of ingredients that can be prepared with little to no thinking. Batch-prep options allow you to make multiple servings at once, so future meals take zero effort.

Repetition-Friendly Meals

Some recipes are designed to be eaten repeatedly without flavor fatigue—ideal for people who prefer eating the same meal every day or struggle with food novelty.

Customization Notes

Every recipe includes options for substitution based on sensory sensitivity, dietary restrictions, or food availability. You'll also find tips on how to adapt meals for texture aversions, spice sensitivities, or ingredient avoidance.

Zero-Pressure Zones

You are not expected to eat three meals a day or cook from scratch every time. Many pages offer simple snack pairings, no-cook foods, or even ideas for eating out or ordering in that are sensory-safe and burnout-compatible.

Eating Through Burnout

Eating during autistic burnout is not simply a matter of hunger or willpower—it's an act of survival and self-preservation. When energy is low, executive dysfunction is high, and the world feels like too much, food can become both a source of comfort and a major challenge.

Many autistic individuals report forgetting to eat, avoiding food due to sensory overwhelm, or defaulting to repetitive, familiar meals. These behaviors are not failures—they're adaptations. Your body is trying to cope, and eating during burnout doesn't need to look like anyone else's idea of healthy. It just needs to be *enough* for you to keep going.

What Happens to the Body During Burnout?

Burnout affects every system of the body. The nervous system becomes dysregulated, making digestion slower or more sensitive. The brain may struggle with planning or initiating tasks like preparing a meal. Sensory thresholds may shift—what once tasted fine may now feel unbearable. The result? Eating can feel confusing, exhausting, or even scary.

That's why during burnout, your goal isn't "perfect nutrition"—it's *sustainable nourishment*. If that means a week of toast and applesauce, that's okay. If it means the same sandwich every day, that's okay too. Eating through burnout means honoring your needs and letting go of shame.

Understanding Sensory-Friendly Nutrition

Sensory-friendly nutrition is an approach that respects the diverse sensory profiles of autistic individuals while still supporting nutritional needs. It means considering not just *what* you eat, but *how* it feels, smells, sounds, and looks—and making food choices that don't overwhelm the senses.

Key Sensory Elements to Consider:

Texture: Some individuals may avoid crunchy, slimy, or gritty foods. Some individuals might favor textures that are soft, creamy, or that dissolve easily in the mouth.

Temperature: Hot foods may feel too intense; cold or room temperature may feel safer and more manageable.

Smell: Strongly aromatic foods may cause nausea or sensory overload.

Flavor: Some may prefer bland or neutral foods; others may crave sour, salty, or sweet tastes.

Appearance: Visually complex or disorganized foods may be unappealing or anxiety-inducing.

Sound: Foods that crunch loudly or sizzle can be distressing to sound-sensitive individuals.

There is no "right" way to eat. If beige foods calm your system, eat beige foods. If you need all your food separated on the plate, honor that. If you prefer one-pot meals because you can't tolerate cleaning multiple dishes, lean into that.

Building a Sensory-Friendly Plate

The foundation of a sensory-friendly meal includes:

A **safe protein**: scrambled eggs, soft tofu, rotisserie chicken, nut butters, or deli meats.

A **soft carb**: rice, pasta, white bread, mashed potatoes, instant oats.

A **familiar fruit or veggie**: cucumber slices, applesauce, baby carrots, peeled apple, steamed broccoli.

A **soothing beverage** might include herbal tea, electrolyte-infused water, warm milk, or fruit juice.

By mixing and matching from sensory-safe categories, you can build a variety of meals without triggering overwhelm.

Safe Foods vs. Challenge Foods

In autistic eating patterns, many individuals distinguish between *safe foods*—those that are predictable, comforting, and easy to eat—and *challenge foods*—those that are unfamiliar, harder to tolerate, or more mentally or physically demanding.

Safe Foods

Safe foods are personal. They are usually:

Predictable in texture and taste

Visually simple or familiar

Easy to prepare or ready-to-eat

Linked to positive associations or routine

Gentle on the digestive system

Examples:

Toast with butter

Cereal with milk

Mashed potatoes

Chicken nuggets

Applesauce

Rice and soy sauce

Why Safe Foods Matter:

Safe foods are a lifeline during burnout. They reduce decision fatigue, provide comfort, and make eating feel possible. Relying on safe foods is not a "bad habit"—it's a valid, functional response to sensory and cognitive overload.

Challenge Foods

Challenge foods are those that may be nutritionally beneficial but are harder to tolerate due to:

Complex textures or strong flavors

Required cooking or prep steps

Unfamiliar presentation

Strong smells or appearances

Examples:

Spicy dishes

Salads with multiple textures

Chewy meats

Mixed dishes (like casseroles)

Strong cheeses or fermented foods

When to Introduce Challenge Foods:

Challenge foods can be introduced gently—*not during the peak of burnout*, but when you feel more regulated. A slow, curiosity-driven approach (like adding one new veggie to a familiar meal) can expand your food range over time without pressure or distress.

Important Reminder:

There is no obligation to "graduate" from safe foods. If your diet is limited, you are still doing your best. You deserve nutrition support without shame. This cookbook includes recipes that use safe foods creatively and provides options for gradual experimentation if and when you're ready.

Tips for Low-Spoon Meal Prep

"Low-spoon" is a term from the Spoon Theory, a framework used by many neurodivergent people to describe energy limits. A "low-spoon" day means you have very little capacity for tasks. On these days, even opening a can or turning on the stove might feel impossible.

Here are practical tips and strategies for eating when you're running on empty:

Stock a Burnout Pantry

Stock your kitchen with easy-to-eat foods that need minimal or no prep. Here are a few suggestions:

Shelf-stable: instant oats, boxed soups, nut butters, applesauce cups, rice cakes, granola bars.

Frozen: pre-cooked rice, microwave veggies, chicken tenders, smoothie packs.

Refrigerated: deli meat, cheese sticks, pre-boiled eggs, hummus, yogurt.

Assemble, Don't Cook

Think of meals as assemblies, not recipes. Examples:

Tortilla + shredded cheese + avocado = wrap

Bread with peanut butter and banana makes a simple open-faced sandwich.

Instant rice mixed with frozen peas and canned tuna creates a quick rice bowl.

Crackers + cheese + grapes = snack plate

Use divided plates or bento boxes to separate textures and reduce sensory overload.

Use Low-Energy Tools

Microwave: reheats or cooks in minutes.

Toaster oven: perfect for small meals.

Electric kettle: quick water for noodles, tea, or oats.

Mini blender: for smoothies or soups.

Pre-cut tools: scissors for herbs or veggies, pre-chopped produce.

Invest in paper plates, pre-cut liners, or dishwasher-safe containers to reduce cleanup stress.

Batch-Prep on High-Spoon Days

When energy is available:

Make big batches of rice, pasta, or soup to freeze in portions.

Prepare fruits and vegetables in advance by chopping or portioning them out.

Freeze sandwiches or burritos that can be microwaved later.

Label food containers by color or sticker to reduce decision-making.

Even prepping *one* thing in advance—like hard-boiling a dozen eggs—can be a huge relief later.

Create Meal Kits or Food Stations

Build pre-assembled "kits" in your fridge or pantry:

Breakfast bin: instant oats, protein bars, fruit.

Lunch drawer: tortilla, hummus, carrots.

Snack tray: crackers, cheese, dried fruit.

Visual organization helps reduce overwhelm. Clear containers or color-coded labels can make it easier to locate food without thinking.

Reduce Decision Fatigue

Eat the same meals multiple times per week.

Rotate 2–3 "default" meals per time of day.

Create a food flowchart: "Do I want hot or cold? Sweet or salty?"

Use a weekly meal grid with no strict times (e.g., pick from any column).

Repetition is not laziness—it's an adaptive strategy.

Accept Support When Available

Ask a friend or family member to prep or drop off meals.

Use grocery delivery or meal services with familiar foods.

Leave post-it instructions if verbal communication is hard.

Communicate preferred food boundaries (textures, smells) to helpers.

There is no shame in outsourcing nourishment.

Burnout strips away energy, but eating does not need to be another source of suffering. Through safe foods, sensory-friendly meals, and low-spoon strategies, you can create a pathway to nourishment that respects your needs.

You are not a failure for needing simplicity. You are not "picky," lazy, or difficult. You are autistic, and your needs are valid.

This book is your toolbox. Let it meet you where you are—and feed you forward.

Pantry & Fridge Essentials

When you're navigating autistic burnout, the kitchen can become a place of overwhelm—but it can also be transformed into a sanctuary of support. A well-stocked pantry and fridge can provide comfort, energy, and sensory-friendly nourishment without requiring major effort. This section will help you build a foundation of ingredients that are versatile, easy to prepare, and attuned to your unique needs.

The Purpose of a Burnout-Friendly Kitchen

The goal is not perfection. It's not about creating gourmet meals or following a strict diet. The goal is to minimize decision-making while making sure you have comforting, nourishing food readily available.

Think of your kitchen as your co-regulator—a place designed to support you when your energy and executive functioning are low. Stocking the right foods in advance is like leaving care packages for your future self.

Staples for Energy and Comfort

Autistic burnout often disrupts your appetite, digestive system, and energy levels. In this state, it's helpful to rely on *energy-dense, easy-to-digest foods* that also offer sensory comfort. Here's a list of practical, burnout-friendly staples to keep on hand.

Pantry Staples

Carbohydrates (Comforting and Easy to Prepare)

Instant rice or microwave rice pouches

Instant mashed potatoes

Pasta or noodles (look for quick-cook or gluten-free if needed)

Instant oatmeal or flavored oats packets

Crackers (saltines, rice crackers, or other preferred textures)

Plain cereals (e.g., cornflakes, Cheerios, puffed rice)

Bread, tortillas, or bagels (can be frozen for long-term storage)

Proteins (Minimal or No Cooking Required)

Canned beans (black beans, chickpeas, lentils)

Canned fish (tuna, salmon, sardines)

Nut butters (peanut, almond, sunflower)

Shelf-stable plant-based milks with protein (soy, pea, almond)

Protein bars or meal replacement shakes

Fruits and Vegetables (Shelf-Stable or Long-Lasting)

Applesauce cups or squeeze pouches

Canned fruit in juice (peaches, pineapple, pears)

Dried fruit (raisins, mango, apricots)

Jarred pasta sauces (for flavor without effort)

Canned vegetables (corn, green beans, carrots)

Soothing Extras

Herbal teas (chamomile, peppermint, ginger)

Broth or bouillon cubes (for sipping or soups)

Honey or maple syrup (gentle sweetness)

Electrolyte drink packets (for hydration and recovery)

Shelf-stable pudding, gelatin cups, or meal shakes

Fridge Essentials

Proteins

Hard-boiled eggs

Sliced cheese or cheese sticks

Deli meats (if tolerated)

Yogurt or Greek yogurt (plain or flavored)

Tofu or tempeh (easy to stir-fry or bake)

Carbs & Sides

Cooked rice or pasta (in clear containers, labeled by day)

Pre-washed salad greens or shredded lettuce

Pre-cut fruit (apple slices, berries, melon)

Leftover portions in single-serve containers

Comfort Foods

Cream cheese, butter, or spreads

Hummus or guacamole

Milk or non-dairy milk

Chia pudding or overnight oats

Freezer Essentials

Pre-cooked frozen rice or grains

Frozen vegetables (peas, corn, carrots, broccoli florets)

Frozen fruit for smoothies

Frozen ready meals (low-sensory, known brands)

Batch-cooked soup, chili, or pasta sauce

Bread, muffins, or pancakes (frozen individually)

Sensory-Friendly Ingredients

When eating during burnout, *how food feels* is often more important than what it is. Sensory-friendly ingredients help reduce overwhelm while still offering nourishment. Below are ingredients categorized by sensory profile.

Mild & Neutral Flavors

White rice

Pasta with butter or plain sauce

Chicken breast or eggs

White bread or plain toast

Mashed potatoes

Oatmeal

Applesauce

Plain crackers or toast

These foods are often described as "safe," "beige," or "non-threatening." They're ideal for low-capacity days.

Soft or Smooth Textures

Yogurt

Mashed sweet potatoes

Hummus

Banana

Avocado

Soft cheese (like cream cheese or mozzarella)

Scrambled eggs

Blended soups

Soft foods require less chewing, are easier to swallow, and can be soothing to an overwhelmed nervous system.

Cold or Room-Temperature Foods

Overnight oats

Smoothies

Cold pasta or rice salads

Cold sandwiches

Chilled fruit or applesauce

Protein shakes

When hot food feels too intense, cold options may be more palatable and quicker to prepare.

Crunchy (but Predictable) Textures

Crackers

Rice cakes

Toasted bread

Carrot sticks

Pretzels

For some, crunchy textures are calming. Choose options that aren't too loud or crumbly, depending on your sensory preferences.

Batch Prep and Storage Tips

On a day when you have a little more energy (a "high-spoon" day), prepping meals or components ahead of time can make burnout days far more manageable. Here's how to do it in a sustainable, non-overwhelming way.

Make a Meal Matrix

Instead of planning strict meals, think in *components*:

Proteins: hard-boiled eggs, canned beans, shredded chicken

Carbs: cooked rice, baked sweet potatoes, pasta

Veggies: roasted carrots, steamed peas, salad greens

Sauces/Dressings: hummus, tahini, olive oil & lemon

Create mix-and-match bowls or plates using these building blocks.

Use Visual and Sensory-Friendly Storage

Store prepped items in clear containers so you can see what's inside.

Label containers with colored tape or day-of-the-week stickers.

Keep the fridge organized by food *type* to reduce search time.

Freeze in Single Servings

Portion soups, rice, or pasta into small containers or freezer bags.

Label with contents and date using a marker.

Freeze flat when possible for easier storage and quicker defrosting.

Batch Cook Low-Sensory Dishes

Ideal recipes include:

Plain rice with peas and tofu

Lentil soup

Mild chicken and vegetable stew

Pasta with butter and grated cheese

Cooking in batches lowers the effort needed for each meal and provides ready-made choices without the need for extra decisions.

Assemble "Snack Plates"

Prepare mini-meal trays in advance:

Crackers + cheese + grapes

Carrot sticks + hummus + pita bread

Rice cakes + nut butter + banana slices

These can be stored in bento boxes and pulled out when you're too tired to think.

6. Make Smoothie Bags

In a freezer-safe bag, combine:

1 banana (peeled)

½ cup frozen berries

Handful of spinach (optional)

1 tbsp flax or chia

When you're ready, mix it with milk or juice to create a full snack or a light meal.

Use Tools That Minimize Cleanup

Use silicone baking mats or parchment paper when preparing meals in the oven.

One-pot or sheet-pan meals for fewer dishes

Lidded bowls that go from fridge to microwave

Make cleaning as effortless as eating.

Feeding yourself during autistic burnout is not just about nutrition—it's about kindness, care, and creating a system that meets *you* where you are. A thoughtfully stocked kitchen full of sensory-friendly ingredients, easy-to-assemble staples, and pre-prepped comfort foods can become your lifeline.

This section is your blueprint to build a kitchen that works *with* your neurology, not against it. Whether you're eating toast three times a day or making batch-prepped bowls once a week, you are feeding your recovery.

You are allowed to need soft food. It's completely okay to eat the same meal each day. You are allowed to rest. You deserve nourishment that aligns with your authentic, everyday needs.q

Comforting Breakfast Recipes

Creamy Banana Oatmeal

Ingredients (1 serving):

½ cup rolled oats

1 cup oat milk (or preferred milk)

1 ripe banana, mashed

1 tsp maple syrup (optional)

Pinch of cinnamon

Instructions:

Place oats and oat milk in a small saucepan.

Heat over medium, stirring now and then, until it begins to simmer.

Add mashed banana and cinnamon. Cook for 5–7 minutes until creamy.

Drizzle with maple syrup if desired.

Nutritional Value (approx.):

Calories: 280 | Carbs: 45g

Protein: 5g | Fat: 7g | Fiber: 6g

Peanut Butter Toast with Applesauce

Ingredients (1 serving):

1 slice whole grain bread

1 tbsp peanut butter

½ cup unsweetened applesauce

Instructions:

Toast bread to preferred crispness.

Spread with peanut butter.

Serve with applesauce on the side or layered on top.

Nutritional Value (approx.):

Calories: 240

Carbs: 27g

Protein: 7g

Fat: 12g

Fiber: 4g

Overnight Chia Pudding

Ingredients (1 serving):

2 tbsp chia seeds

½ cup almond milk

½ tsp vanilla extract

1 tsp honey or maple syrup

Optional: sliced strawberries or banana

Instructions:

Mix chia seeds, milk, vanilla, and sweetener in a jar or bowl.

Mix thoroughly, then chill in the fridge overnight or for a minimum of 2 hours.

Top with fruit before serving.

Nutritional Value (approx.):

Calories: 190

Carbs: 14g

Protein: 5g

Fat: 11g | Fiber: 9g

Yogurt with Soft Berries and Granola

Ingredients (1 serving):

¾ cup plain Greek yogurt

¼ cup soft blueberries or raspberries

2 tbsp low-sugar granola

Instructions:

Spoon yogurt into a bowl.

Gently fold in berries.

Top with granola (or serve on the side if crunch is overstimulating).

Nutritional Value (approx.):

Calories: 220

Carbs: 18g

Protein: 14g

Fat: 9g

Fiber: 3g

Soft Scrambled Eggs and Toast

Ingredients (1 serving):

2 eggs

1 tbsp milk

1 tsp butter

1 slice soft bread

Instructions:

Beat eggs with milk.

Heat a nonstick pan on low and let the butter melt gently.

Add eggs and gently stir until just set and soft.

Serve with warm toast.

Nutritional Value (approx.):

Calories: 290

Carbs: 12g

Protein: 14g

Fat: 20g | Fiber: 1g

Applesauce Pancakes (Mini-Batch)

Ingredients (1 serving, ~3 pancakes):

½ cup of pancake mix (or substitute with ¼ cup flour and a small pinch of baking powder)

¼ cup unsweetened applesauce

1 tbsp milk or water

Butter or oil for cooking

Instructions:

Mix pancake ingredients into a smooth batter.

Heat a nonstick pan on medium and lightly oil.

Spoon out small amounts of batter and cook for 2–3 minutes on each side.

Serve plain or with a touch of syrup.

Nutritional Value (approx.):

Calories: 210

Carbs: 35g

Protein: 4g

Fat: 6g | Fiber: 2g

Creamy Avocado Toast

Ingredients (1 serving):

1 slice soft whole grain or white bread

½ ripe avocado

Pinch of salt

Optional: squeeze of lemon or mashed white beans

Instructions:

Toast bread lightly.

Mash avocado with salt (and lemon/beans if using).

Spread onto toast and slice into strips if helpful.

Nutritional Value (approx.):

Calories: 250

Carbs: 18g

Protein: 4g

Fat: 18g

Fiber: 7g

Rice Porridge (Congee-Style)

Ingredients (1 serving):

½ cup cooked white rice

1 cup water or broth

Pinch of salt

Optional: soft tofu cubes or shredded chicken

Instructions:

In a pot, combine cooked rice and water.

Simmer over low heat 10–15 minutes until creamy.

Stir occasionally, adding more water if needed.

Add protein if desired.

Nutritional Value (approx.):

Calories: 170 (base)

Carbs: 35g

Protein: 3g

Fat: 1g | Fiber: 1g

Banana & Oat Smoothie

Ingredients (1 serving):

1 ripe banana

½ cup oat milk

2 tbsp rolled oats

1 tsp flaxseed or chia (optional)

½ tsp cinnamon

Instructions:

Add all ingredients to a blender.

Blend until smooth and creamy.

Serve chilled.

Nutritional Value (approx.):

Calories: 220

Carbs: 38g

Protein: 4g

Fat: 5g | Fiber: 5g

Cottage Cheese and Pear Bowl

Ingredients (1 serving):

½ cup cottage cheese

½ ripe pear, peeled and chopped

1 tsp honey (optional)

Dash of cinnamon

Instructions:

Scoop cottage cheese into a bowl.

Top with pear and drizzle of honey.

Sprinkle with cinnamon if using.

Nutritional Value (approx.):

Calories: 180

Carbs: 16g

Protein: 12g

Fat: 7g

Fiber: 2g

Soothing Lunch Recipes

Creamy Mashed Potato Bowl with Soft Peas

Ingredients (1 serving):

1 medium potato (150g), peeled and cubed

1 tbsp butter

2 tbsp milk

½ cup frozen peas

Salt to taste

Instructions:

Boil potatoes until fork-tender (about 15 minutes).

Drain and mash with butter and milk.

Steam the peas in a different pot for 5–7 minutes until they're tender.

Mash peas lightly if needed. Serve side by side or combined.

Nutrition (approx.):

Calories: 290 | Carbs: 42g

Protein: 6g | Fat: 11g | Fiber: 5g

Soft Rice with Steamed Carrots and Tofu

Ingredients (1 serving):

½ cup cooked white rice

½ cup diced carrots

½ cup soft tofu, cubed

1 tsp soy sauce (optional)

Instructions:

Steam carrots until soft (10–12 minutes).

Gently warm rice and tofu.

Combine all, drizzle with soy sauce if desired.

Nutrition (approx.):

Calories: 260

Carbs: 35g

Protein: 10g

Fat: 7g

Fiber: 4g

Mild Chicken and Rice Soup

Ingredients (1 serving):

½ cup cooked shredded chicken

¾ cup cooked rice

1 ½ cups low-sodium chicken broth

¼ cup soft-cooked diced carrots

Pinch of salt

Instructions:

Combine all ingredients in a small pot.

Simmer 5–10 minutes until warm and soft.

Mash slightly if preferred smoother.

Nutrition (approx.):

Calories: 330

Carbs: 28g

Protein: 25g

Fat: 10g | Fiber: 2g

Scrambled Egg Rice Bowl

Ingredients (1 serving):

2 eggs

½ cup cooked rice

1 tsp butter

1 tsp low-sodium soy sauce (optional)

Instructions:

Gently cook scrambled eggs in butter on low heat until they're soft and tender.

Gently mix with rice and soy sauce.

Serve warm in a bowl.

Nutrition (approx.):

Calories: 310

Carbs: 26g

Protein: 14g

Fat: 18g

Fiber: 1g

Creamy Lentil Mash with Soft Bread

Ingredients (1 serving):

½ cup cooked red lentils

1 tsp olive oil

Pinch of cumin (optional)

1 slice soft bread

Instructions:

Cook red lentils until mushy (about 15–20 minutes).

Stir in olive oil and season if desired.

Serve with soft bread or mash together.

Nutrition (approx.):

Calories: 270

Carbs: 32g

Protein: 12g

Fat: 9g

Fiber: 8g

Baked Sweet Potato with Cottage Cheese

Ingredients (1 serving):

1 medium sweet potato (200g)

½ cup cottage cheese

Dash of cinnamon or salt

Instructions:

Cook the sweet potato in the oven at 400°F (200°C) for 45 minutes, or microwave it for 5 to 7 minutes.

Cut open and fill with cottage cheese.

Sprinkle cinnamon or salt if desired.

Nutrition (approx.):

Calories: 290

Carbs: 36g

Protein: 13g

Fat: 9g

Fiber: 6g

Smooth Tuna Rice Salad

Ingredients (1 serving):

½ cup cooked white rice

½ can tuna in water, drained

1 tbsp plain Greek yogurt or mayo

1 tsp lemon juice (optional)

Instructions:

Mix tuna with yogurt/mayo and lemon juice.

Combine with rice for a soft, scoopable salad.

Chill or serve warm.

Nutrition (approx.):

Calories: 300

Carbs: 28g

Protein: 20g

Fat: 11g

Fiber: 1g

Soft Pasta with Avocado Sauce

Ingredients (1 serving):

½ cup cooked small pasta (e.g., shells)

½ ripe avocado

1 tsp olive oil

Pinch of garlic powder (optional)

Instructions:

Blend avocado with olive oil and garlic powder.

Stir into warm pasta until creamy.

Serve immediately.

Nutrition (approx.):

Calories: 330

Carbs: 32g

Protein: 6g

Fat: 21g

Fiber: 6g

Silky Polenta with Soft Vegetables

Ingredients (1 serving):

½ cup quick-cook polenta

1 ½ cups water or broth

1 tsp butter

½ cup steamed zucchini or carrots

Instructions:

Bring liquid to boil, stir in polenta, reduce heat.

Cook 5 minutes, stirring constantly.

Add butter and mix in vegetables.

Nutrition (approx.):

Calories: 280

Carbs: 38g

Protein: 5g

Fat: 11g

Fiber: 3g

Soft Egg Salad Wrap

Ingredients (1 serving):

2 boiled eggs, mashed

1 tbsp mayo or plain yogurt

1 soft whole wheat tortilla

Salt to taste

Instructions:

Mash eggs with mayo/yogurt and a pinch of salt.

Spread onto tortilla and fold gently.

Optionally warm in microwave for 10 seconds.

Nutrition (approx.):

Calories: 320

Carbs: 22g

Protein: 14g

Fat: 20g

Fiber: 2g

Low-Effort, Soothing Dinner Recipes

Cheesy Rice and Broccoli Bowl

Ingredients (1 serving):

½ cup cooked white rice

½ cup steamed broccoli (chopped small)

2 tbsp shredded mild cheddar cheese

1 tsp olive oil

Instructions:

Combine rice, broccoli, and cheese in a bowl.

Microwave for 1–2 minutes until cheese melts.

Stir in olive oil and serve warm.

Nutrition (approx.):

Calories: 280

Carbs: 30g

Protein: 9g

Fat: 13g | Fiber: 3g

Soft Egg Noodles with Butter and Peas

Ingredients (1 serving):

1 cup cooked egg noodles

½ cup frozen peas

1 tbsp butter

Salt to taste

Instructions:

Microwave or boil peas until soft.

Mix warm noodles, peas, and butter.

Add salt to taste and serve.

Nutrition (approx.):

Calories: 340

Carbs: 39g

Protein: 10g

Fat: 16g

Fiber: 4g

Baked Potato with Greek Yogurt and Chives

Ingredients (1 serving):

1 medium russet potato (200g)

2 tbsp plain Greek yogurt

1 tsp chopped chives

Pinch of salt

Instructions:

Microwave or bake potato until soft (5–10 mins).

Cut open and fluff with a fork.

Top with yogurt, chives, and salt.

Nutrition (approx.):

Calories: 250

Carbs: 38g

Protein: 8g

Fat: 6g

Fiber: 4g

Soft Tofu Stir (No-Fry) Bowl

Ingredients (1 serving):

½ cup soft tofu, cubed

½ cup cooked jasmine rice

¼ cup shredded carrot

1 tsp low-sodium soy sauce

Instructions:

Lightly combine the tofu, rice, and carrots in a bowl.

Drizzle soy sauce over and microwave 1–2 minutes.

Serve warm or at room temperature.

Nutrition (approx.):

Calories: 260

Carbs: 28g

Protein: 12g

Fat: 10g

Fiber: 2g

Creamy Pumpkin Soup with Toasted Bread

Ingredients (1 serving):

1 cup canned pumpkin puree

¾ cup low-sodium vegetable broth

2 tbsp plain cream or oat milk

1 slice soft whole grain bread

Instructions:

Heat pumpkin, broth, and cream in a pot for 5 minutes.

Blend for smoother texture if needed.

Serve with soft bread for dipping.

Nutrition (approx.):

Calories: 230

Carbs: 28g

Protein: 5g

Fat: 10g

Fiber: 5g

Chicken and Mashed Cauliflower

Ingredients (1 serving):

½ cup shredded rotisserie chicken

1 cup steamed cauliflower

1 tbsp butter or olive oil

Salt to taste

Instructions:

Steam cauliflower until very soft.

Mash with butter and a pinch of salt.

Add warm chicken on top.

Nutrition (approx.):

Calories: 280

Carbs: 10g

Protein: 22g

Fat: 18g

Fiber: 3g

Soft Polenta with Mushrooms

Ingredients (1 serving):

½ cup instant polenta

1 ½ cups water or broth

¼ cup finely chopped mushrooms

1 tsp olive oil

Instructions:

Simmer polenta in the liquid for 5 minutes, stirring continuously.

Meanwhile, sauté mushrooms in olive oil in another pan or soften them in the microwave.

Combine and serve warm.

Nutrition (approx.):

Calories: 270

Carbs: 35g

Protein: 5g

Fat: 12g

Fiber: 2g

Turkey and Sweet Potato Mash

Ingredients (1 serving):

½ cup ground turkey, cooked

1 medium sweet potato (200g), mashed

1 tsp olive oil

Salt to taste

Instructions:

Microwave sweet potato until soft (5–6 mins). Mash with olive oil.

Warm turkey and mix into mash or serve on the side.

Add salt if desired.

Nutrition (approx.):

Calories: 330

Carbs: 28g

Protein: 20g

Fat: 15g

Fiber: 5g

Quinoa with Steamed Zucchini and Parmesan

Ingredients (1 serving):

½ cup cooked quinoa

½ cup zucchini, steamed and chopped

1 tbsp grated parmesan cheese

1 tsp olive oil

Instructions:

Steam zucchini until soft (6–8 minutes).

Mix with quinoa, parmesan, and olive oil.

Serve warm in a bowl.

Nutrition (approx.):

Calories: 290

Carbs: 26g

Protein: 10g

Fat: 16g

Fiber: 4g

Creamy Avocado Pasta

Ingredients (1 serving):

½ cup small cooked pasta (e.g., shells)

½ ripe avocado

1 tbsp lemon juice

1 tsp olive oil

Pinch of garlic powder (optional)

Instructions:

Mash avocado with lemon juice, olive oil, and garlic powder.

Mix into warm pasta until smooth and creamy.

Serve immediately.

Nutrition (approx.):

Calories: 350

Carbs: 30g

Protein: 6g

Fat: 24g | Fiber: 7g

Safe Snacks and Quick Bites Recipes

Banana and Peanut Butter Wrap

Ingredients (1 serving):

1 small tortilla (whole wheat or plain)

1 medium banana

1 tbsp smooth peanut butter

Instructions:

Spread peanut butter on tortilla.

Position the peeled banana at one end and roll it up.

Slice in half or eat whole.

Nutrition (approx.):

Calories: 290

Carbs: 32g

Protein: 7g

Fat: 16g

Fiber: 5g

Yogurt and Applesauce Swirl

Ingredients (1 serving):

½ cup plain or vanilla Greek yogurt

¼ cup unsweetened applesauce

Optional: cinnamon pinch

Instructions:

Mix yogurt and applesauce in a bowl.

Add a pinch of cinnamon if desired.

Eat with spoon or chilled.

Nutrition (approx.):

Calories: 150

Carbs: 18g

Protein: 10g

Fat: 3g

Fiber: 2g

Rice Cake with Cream Cheese and Cucumber

Ingredients (1 serving):

1 plain rice cake

1 tbsp plain cream cheese

3–4 thin cucumber slices

Instructions:

Spread cream cheese on rice cake.

Top with cucumber slices.

Eat immediately before rice cake softens.

Nutrition (approx.):

Calories: 100

Carbs: 10g

Protein: 2g

Fat: 6g

Fiber: 1g

Soft-Boiled Egg and Toast Strips

Ingredients (1 serving):

1 egg

1 slice soft bread

Instructions:

Boil egg for 6 minutes for soft yolk.

Slice bread into strips.

Dip toast strips in egg yolk or eat on the side.

Nutrition (approx.):

Calories: 180

Carbs: 12g

Protein: 9g

Fat: 10g

Fiber: 1g

Cheese Cubes and Plain Crackers

Ingredients (1 serving):

4 whole grain or plain crackers

1 oz mild cheddar or mozzarella cheese, cubed

Instructions:

Arrange cheese cubes and crackers on a plate.

Eat with fingers or a toothpick.

Nutrition (approx.):

Calories: 220

Carbs: 15g

Protein: 9g

Fat: 13g

Fiber: 2g

Smooth Apples and Oats Bite Bowl

Ingredients (1 serving):

½ apple, peeled and finely chopped

2 tbsp rolled oats

1 tbsp almond or peanut butter

1 tsp honey (optional)

Instructions:

Mix all ingredients in a bowl.

Microwave for 20–30 seconds if softer texture preferred.

Stir and serve with spoon.

Nutrition (approx.):

Calories: 210

Carbs: 26g

Protein: 5g

Fat: 10g

Fiber: 4g

Mild Tuna and Mayo Toast

Ingredients (1 serving):

½ can (2 oz) of drained, mild-smelling tuna packed in water

1 tsp mayonnaise

1 slice soft bread

Instructions:

Mix tuna and mayo in a bowl.

Spread on bread.

Eat as is or toast lightly if preferred.

Nutrition (approx.):

Calories: 190

Carbs: 12g

Protein: 14g

Fat: 10g

Fiber: 1g

Oat and Banana Soft Bites (No-Bake)

Ingredients (makes 3 bites):

½ ripe banana

¼ cup quick oats

1 tsp maple syrup or honey

Instructions:

Mash banana in a bowl.

Mix in oats and syrup.

Form into 3 soft balls. Chill or eat immediately.

Nutrition per serving (3 bites):

Calories: 160

Carbs: 27g

Protein: 3g

Fat: 3g

Fiber: 3g

Avocado and Rice Cake Mash

Ingredients (1 serving):

1 rice cake

¼ ripe avocado

Pinch of salt

Instructions:

Mash avocado in a bowl.

Spread on rice cake and sprinkle with salt.

Eat promptly for best texture.

Nutrition (approx.):

Calories: 160

Carbs: 12g

Protein: 2g

Fat: 12g

Fiber: 4g

Cottage Cheese with Soft Pear Chunks

Ingredients (1 serving):

½ cup cottage cheese

½ soft ripe pear, peeled and chopped

Instructions:

Scoop cottage cheese into bowl.

Add chopped pear on top or stir in.

Eat cold with spoon.

Nutrition (approx.):

Calories: 170

Carbs: 15g

Protein: 12g

Fat: 7g

Fiber: 2g

Calming Drinks & Smoothies

Banana Oat Smoothie

Ingredients (1 serving):

1 medium banana

½ cup oat milk

¼ cup rolled oats

½ tsp vanilla extract

Optional: ½ tsp honey

Instructions:

Add all ingredients to a blender.

Blend until smooth (30–45 seconds).

Serve immediately or chill.

Nutrition (approx.):

Calories: 230 | Carbs: 38g

Protein: 4g | Fat: 5g | Fiber: 5g

Warm Chamomile Vanilla Milk

Ingredients (1 serving):

1 chamomile tea bag

¾ cup hot water

¼ cup warm almond milk

¼ tsp vanilla extract

Instructions:

Steep tea in hot water for 5 minutes.

Stir in warm almond milk and vanilla.

Sip warm.

Nutrition (approx.):

Calories: 25

Carbs: 3g

Protein: 1g

Fat: 1g

Fiber: 0g

Creamy Coconut-Date Smoothie

Ingredients (1 serving):

1 cup unsweetened coconut milk

2 soft Medjool dates, pitted

½ frozen banana

¼ tsp cinnamon

Instructions:

Blend all ingredients until fully smooth.

Serve chilled.

Nutrition (approx.):

Calories: 220

Carbs: 30g

Protein: 2g

Fat: 12g

Fiber: 4g

Gentle Green Smoothie

Ingredients (1 serving):

½ banana

½ cup spinach (fresh or frozen)

½ cup oat or almond milk

1 tbsp plain yogurt

Optional: 1 tsp maple syrup

Instructions:

Blend until green and creamy.

Chill or drink right away.

Nutrition (approx.):

Calories: 140

Carbs: 18g

Protein: 4g

Fat: 6g

Fiber: 3g

Lavender Honey Milk (Warm or Cold)

Ingredients (1 serving):

1 cup milk (dairy or plant-based)

½ tsp dried culinary lavender

½ tsp honey

Instructions:

Warm milk gently with lavender (don't boil).

Let steep for 3–5 minutes.

Strain, stir in honey, and serve.

Nutrition (approx.):

Calories: 120

Carbs: 13g

Protein: 3g

Fat: 6g

Fiber: 0g

Berry Yogurt Smoothie

Ingredients (1 serving):

½ cup frozen mixed berries

½ cup plain Greek yogurt

¼ cup milk or water

Optional: ½ tsp chia seeds

Instructions:

Blend until smooth and creamy.

Serve cold with a spoon or straw.

Nutrition (approx.):

Calories: 170

Carbs: 18g

Protein: 10g

Fat: 5g

Fiber: 3g

Warm Apple Cider Soother

Ingredients (1 serving):

¾ cup apple juice

¼ tsp cinnamon

1 tsp lemon juice

Instructions:

Warm apple juice gently on stovetop.

Stir in cinnamon and lemon juice.

Sip slowly while warm.

Nutrition (approx.):

Calories: 90

Carbs: 22g

Protein: 0g

Fat: 0g

Fiber: 0g

Silky Almond-Date Milkshake

Ingredients (1 serving):

1 cup almond milk

2 Medjool dates

½ tsp vanilla extract

Pinch of sea salt

Instructions:

Soak dates in warm water 5 minutes if needed.

Blend everything until smooth.

Drink slowly or chill before sipping.

Nutrition (approx.):

Calories: 160

Carbs: 25g

Protein: 2g

Fat: 6g

Fiber: 3g

Cooling Cucumber-Mint Water

Ingredients (1 serving):

1 cup cold water

3 cucumber slices

2 fresh mint leaves

Instructions:

Add cucumber and mint to water.

Chill for 10+ minutes before drinking.

Strain if desired.

Nutrition (approx.):

Calories: 5

Carbs: 1g

Protein: 0g

Fat: 0g

Fiber: 0g

Simple Vanilla Oat Drink

Ingredients (1 serving):

½ cup cooked oats

1 cup water or oat milk

¼ tsp vanilla extract

Optional: dash cinnamon or maple syrup

Instructions:

Blend cooked oats with water or oat milk.

Add vanilla and blend again.

Drink warm or chilled.

Nutrition (approx.):

Calories: 130

Carbs: 22g

Protein: 3g

Fat: 3g

Fiber: 3g

Comforting Dessert Recipes

Soft Banana Chia Pudding

Ingredients (2 servings):

1 ripe banana

1 cup unsweetened almond milk

3 tbsp chia seeds

½ tsp vanilla extract

Instructions:

Mash banana in a bowl until smooth.

Stir in almond milk, chia seeds, and vanilla.

Refrigerate for at least 4 hours or overnight.

Stir well before serving.

Nutrition (per serving):

Calories: 160 | Carbs: 23g

Protein: 3g | Fat: 7g | Fiber: 6g

Applesauce Yogurt Parfait

Ingredients (1 serving):

½ cup unsweetened applesauce

½ cup plain Greek yogurt

1 tsp maple syrup (optional)

Pinch of cinnamon

Instructions:

In a glass or bowl, layer yogurt and applesauce.

Drizzle with maple syrup and sprinkle cinnamon.

Chill for 10 minutes or eat immediately.

Nutrition:

Calories: 130

Carbs: 16g

Protein: 8g

Fat: 3g

Fiber: 1g

Creamy Rice Pudding (Dairy-Free Option)

Ingredients (2 servings):

½ cup cooked white rice

1 cup almond milk

1 tbsp maple syrup

¼ tsp cinnamon

½ tsp vanilla extract

Instructions:

In a saucepan, combine all ingredients.

Simmer on low heat for 10–12 minutes, stirring frequently.

Serve warm or cold.

Nutrition (per serving):

Calories: 160

Carbs: 28g

Protein: 2g

Fat: 4g | Fiber: 1g

Baked Pear with Cinnamon

Ingredients (1 serving):

1 ripe pear, halved and cored

¼ tsp cinnamon

½ tsp coconut oil or butter

Instructions:

Preheat oven to 350°F (175°C).

Place pear halves on a baking dish.

Top each with a bit of cinnamon and coconut oil.

Bake for 20–25 minutes until soft.

Nutrition:

Calories: 110

Carbs: 27g

Protein: 1g

Fat: 3g

Fiber: 4g

Soothing Mango Mousse

Ingredients (2 servings):

1 cup chopped ripe mango

½ cup plain Greek yogurt or coconut yogurt

1 tsp honey (optional)

Instructions:

Blend all ingredients until smooth and fluffy.

Chill for 30 minutes before serving.

Nutrition (per serving):

Calories: 130

Carbs: 22g

Protein: 4g

Fat: 3g

Fiber: 2g

Coconut Date Balls

Ingredients (6 balls):

6 Medjool dates, pitted

¼ cup shredded coconut

2 tbsp sunflower seed butter or almond butter

½ tsp vanilla extract

Instructions:

Blend all ingredients in a food processor.

Form into 6 small balls with damp hands.

Chill for 30 minutes before eating.

Nutrition (per ball):

Calories: 90

Carbs: 12g

Protein: 1g

Fat: 4g

Fiber: 2g

Oatmeal Cookie Mug Cake (Microwave)

Ingredients (1 serving):

2 tbsp oat flour

1 tbsp applesauce

1 tbsp maple syrup

¼ tsp cinnamon

Pinch of baking soda

Instructions:

Mix everything in a microwave-safe mug.

Microwave on high for 60–90 seconds.

Cool slightly and enjoy.

Nutrition:

Calories: 150

Carbs: 28g

Protein: 2g

Fat: 3g | Fiber: 2g

Melty Chocolate Banana Bites

Ingredients (4 bites):

1 banana, sliced into thick rounds

2 tbsp dark chocolate chips (dairy-free if needed)

Instructions:

Microwave chocolate chips in 15-second bursts until melted.

Dip banana slices halfway into chocolate.

Chill for 10 minutes on wax paper.

Nutrition (per bite):

Calories: 45

Carbs: 9g

Protein: 0.5g

Fat: 2g

Fiber: 1g

Warm Apples with Cinnamon Oats

Ingredients (1 serving):

½ apple, diced

½ cup cooked oats

¼ tsp cinnamon

1 tsp maple syrup

Instructions:

Heat apple in a small pan until soft.

Stir in oats, cinnamon, and maple syrup.

Serve warm in a bowl.

Nutrition:

Calories: 180

Carbs: 32g

Protein: 4g

Fat: 3g

Fiber: 4g

Frozen Yogurt Bark with Berries

Ingredients (4 pieces):

½ cup plain or vanilla Greek yogurt

¼ cup mixed berries (frozen or fresh)

1 tsp honey

Instructions:

Spread yogurt on a lined tray.

Scatter berries and drizzle with honey.

Freeze for 2+ hours, then break into pieces.

Nutrition (per piece):

Calories: 40

Carbs: 5g

Protein: 2g

Fat: 1g

Fiber: 0.5g

Hydration-friendly broth Recipes

Simple Vegetable Mineral Broth

Ingredients (4 cups):

1 large carrot, chopped (100g)

1 celery stalk, chopped (80g)

1 small onion, quartered (80g)

1 garlic clove, smashed

4 cups water

1 tbsp olive oil

Pinch of sea salt

Instructions:

Warm olive oil in a pot and cook the vegetables for 3–4 minutes, stirring occasionally.

Add water and bring to a boil.

Simmer uncovered for 30 minutes.

Strain and serve warm.

Nutrition (per cup):

Calories: 30 | Carbs: 6g | Protein: 0.5g

Fat: 1.5g | Sodium: 120mg

Ginger-Turmeric Healing Broth

Ingredients (4 cups):

4 cups water

1-inch piece of fresh ginger, sliced

½ tsp ground turmeric or 1-inch turmeric root

1 tbsp lemon juice

½ tsp sea salt

Optional: 1 tsp honey for a soothing finish

Instructions:

Gently simmer the ginger and turmeric in water for 15 to 20 minutes.

Strain, stir in lemon juice and salt.

Serve warm, optionally with honey.

Nutrition (per cup):

Calories: 10 | Carbs: 2g

Protein: 0g | Fat: 0g

Sodium: 150mg

Coconut-Lime Broth

Ingredients (2 cups):

1 cup water

1 cup light coconut milk

Juice of ½ lime

Pinch of salt

1 tsp grated ginger

Instructions:

Simmer all ingredients gently for 5–10 minutes.

Strain if preferred and serve warm.

Nutrition (per cup):

Calories: 80

Carbs: 3g

Protein: 0g

Fat: 7g

Sodium: 160mg

Bone Broth with Carrot & Parsley

Ingredients (4 cups):

4 cups chicken or beef bone broth (store-bought or homemade)

1 carrot, grated

1 tbsp chopped fresh parsley

Instructions:

Heat bone broth in a saucepan.

Add grated carrot and simmer for 10 minutes.

Stir in parsley before serving.

Nutrition (per cup):

Calories: 60

Carbs: 3g

Protein: 6g

Fat: 3g

Sodium: 300mg

Miso-Ginger Broth

Ingredients (2 cups):

2 cups water

1 tbsp white miso paste

½ tsp grated ginger

Optional: ¼ sheet nori, shredded

Instructions:

Warm the water and ginger until it's hot, but not boiling.

Stir in miso paste until fully dissolved.

Add nori if desired.

Nutrition (per cup):

Calories: 35

Carbs: 5g

Protein: 2g

Fat: 1g

Sodium: 450mg

Soothing Cucumber-Peppermint Broth (Chilled Option)

Ingredients (2 cups):

1 cucumber, peeled and blended

2 cups water

1 tsp dried mint or a few fresh mint leaves

Pinch of salt

Instructions:

Combine all ingredients in a pitcher.

Let steep in the fridge for 1 hour.

Strain and serve chilled.

Nutrition (per cup):

Calories: 8

Carbs: 2g

Protein: 0.5g

Fat: 0g | Sodium: 50mg

Mushroom Umami Broth

Ingredients (4 cups):

½ cup dried shiitake mushrooms

4 cups water

1 tbsp tamari or low-sodium soy sauce

½ tsp garlic powder

Instructions:

Soak mushrooms in water for 30 minutes.

Cook the soaked mushrooms and their liquid with tamari and garlic powder at a simmer for 20 minutes.

Strain and serve.

Nutrition (per cup):

Calories: 25

Carbs: 3g

Protein: 2g

Fat: 0g

Sodium: 250mg

Hydration Broth with Electrolytes

Ingredients (4 cups):

4 cups water

½ tsp salt

¼ tsp potassium salt (like LoSalt)

1 tbsp lemon juice

1 tsp maple syrup (optional)

Instructions:

Warm all ingredients in a saucepan, stir until salts dissolve.

Serve warm or sip cooled.

Nutrition (per cup):

Calories: 10 | Carbs: 2g

Protein: 0g

Fat: 0g

Sodium: 300mg

Potassium: 150mg

Fennel & Chamomile Digestive Broth

Ingredients (2 cups):

1 tsp fennel seeds

1 chamomile tea bag

2 cups boiling water

Pinch of salt

Instructions:

Place the fennel seeds and tea bag into the hot water.

Steep for 10–15 minutes.

Strain and add salt before drinking.

Nutrition (per cup):

Calories: 5

Carbs: 1g

Protein: 0g

Fat: 0g

Sodium: 80mg

Sweet Potato Comfort Broth

Ingredients (2 cups):

½ small sweet potato, peeled and diced (75g)

2 cups vegetable broth

Pinch of cinnamon

Optional: 1 tsp coconut oil

Instructions:

Cook the diced sweet potato in broth at a simmer for 15–20 minutes.

Blend if preferred for a smooth texture.

Add cinnamon and coconut oil if using.

Nutrition (per cup):

Calories: 65

Carbs: 10g

Protein: 1g

Fat: 3g

Sodium: 220mg

Bonus: 28-Days Autistic Burnout Meal Plan for Recovery

Day 1 to Day 7: Grounding & Stabilizing

Day 1

Breakfast: Banana Oat Mash

Lunch: Gentle Rice Bowl with Steamed Carrots

Dinner: Slow Cooker Lentil Stew

Snack: Applesauce with Cinnamon

Drink: Warm Chamomile Banana Milk

Broth: Simple Vegetable Mineral Broth

Day 2

Breakfast: Soft Scrambled Eggs with Toast Fingers

Lunch: Mashed Sweet Potato Bowl

Dinner: One-Pot Creamy Rice with Zucchini

Snack: Plain Yogurt with Honey

Drink: Cucumber-Lime Water

Broth: Bone Broth with Carrot & Parsley

Day 3

Breakfast: Rice Porridge with Pear

Lunch: Smooth Avocado-Pea Soup

Dinner: Baked Sweet Potato with Tahini Drizzle

Snack: Rice Cakes with Almond Butter

Drink: Coconut Banana Smoothie

Broth: Ginger-Turmeric Healing Broth

Day 4

Breakfast: Chia Pudding with Apples

Lunch: Hummus Wrap (soft tortilla)

Dinner: Lazy Pasta with Olive Oil and Garlic

Snack: Frozen Blueberry Bites

Drink: Warm Oat Milk with Maple

Broth: Mushroom Umami Broth

Day 5

Breakfast: Applesauce Pancakes

Lunch: Creamy Carrot-Coconut Soup

Dinner: Stuffed Baked Potato with Broccoli

Snack: Soft Granola Bites

Drink: Cucumber Mint Smoothie

Broth: Miso-Ginger Broth

Day 6

Breakfast: Yogurt with Warm Berries

Lunch: Plain Pasta with Butter and Peas

Dinner: Egg Fried Rice (low seasoning)

Snack: Boiled Egg with Sea Salt

Drink: Turmeric Coconut Latte

Broth: Fennel & Chamomile Digestive Broth

Day 7

Breakfast: Creamy Banana Rice

Lunch: Lentil Mash with Steamed Spinach

Dinner: Tomato Rice Casserole

Snack: Fruit Leather or Soft Dates

Drink: Oat Milk Cinnamon Shake

Broth: Coconut-Lime Broth

Day 8 to Day 14: Nourishing & Balancing

Day 8

Breakfast: Overnight Oats with Banana

Lunch: Mashed Chickpea Wrap

Dinner: Baked Zucchini with Quinoa

Snack: Roasted Carrot Sticks

Drink: Warm Lemon Honey Water

Broth: Sweet Potato Comfort Broth

Day 9

Breakfast: Rice Cakes with Cottage Cheese

Lunch: Soft Tofu Stir Fry (minimal oil)

Dinner: Roasted Pumpkin Bowl

Snack: Apples with Peanut Butter

Drink: Herbal Berry Cooler

Broth: Simple Vegetable Mineral Broth

Day 10

Breakfast: Warm Millet Porridge

Lunch: Zucchini Cream Soup

Dinner: Turkey and Rice Bake

Snack: Plain Popcorn

Drink: Banana Almond Smoothie

Broth: Ginger-Turmeric Healing Broth

Day 11

Breakfast: Toast with Ghee and Cinnamon

Lunch: Avocado and Brown Rice Bowl

Dinner: Chickpea Mash with Carrots

Snack: Soft Cucumber Rounds

Drink: Warm Peppermint Milk

Broth: Mushroom Umami Broth

Day 12

Breakfast: Yogurt Chia Bowl

Lunch: Quinoa with Steamed Green Beans

Dinner: Soft-Cooked Lentil Pasta

Snack: Banana Bites with Sunflower Seed Butter

Drink: Strawberry Coconut Water Smoothie

Broth: Miso-Ginger Broth

Day 13

Breakfast: Soft Banana Muffins

Lunch: Rice Noodle Soup with Peas

Dinner: Creamy Polenta with Carrot Purée

Snack: Applesauce and Oats Cookies

Drink: Gentle Lavender Oat Latte

Broth: Fennel & Chamomile Digestive Broth

Day 14

Breakfast: Creamy Rice Cereal

Lunch: Mashed Potatoes with Spinach Puree

Dinner: Roasted Butternut Squash and Rice

Snack: Plain Rice Crackers

Drink: Oat Milk Honey Blend

Broth: Bone Broth with Carrot & Parsley

Day 15 to Day 21: Comfort & Strength

Day 15

Breakfast: Warm Cinnamon Quinoa

Lunch: Sweet Potato Chickpea Bowl

Dinner: Soft Rice Casserole with Lentils

Snack: Banana Oat Bites

Drink: Carob Banana Smoothie

Broth: Coconut-Lime Broth

Day 16

Breakfast: Simple Scrambled Tofu

Lunch: Broccoli Mash with Millet

Dinner: Veggie Ramen (low-spice)

Snack: Apple Slices and Tahini

Drink: Cucumber-Lemon Herbal Water

Broth: Hydration Broth with Electrolytes

Day 17

Breakfast: Toast with Avocado

Lunch: Zucchini Fritters (baked)

Dinner: Soft Baked Pasta with Butternut Sauce

Snack: Cooled Edamame with Salt

Drink: Warm Spiced Apple Smoothie

Broth: Ginger-Turmeric Healing Broth

Day 18

Breakfast: Rice Porridge with Blueberries

Lunch: Carrot-Lentil Mash

Dinner: Baked Cauliflower Rice Bowl

Snack: Chia and Yogurt Bowl

Drink: Banana-Date Smoothie

Broth: Mushroom Umami Broth

Day 19

Breakfast: Creamy Coconut Oatmeal

Lunch: Chickpea Wrap with Mashed Avocado

Dinner: Baked Potato and Veggie Bowl

Snack: Soft Boiled Egg

Drink: Vanilla Almond Smoothie

Broth: Sweet Potato Comfort Broth

Day 20

Breakfast: Applesauce Overnight Oats

Lunch: Rice and Soft Bean Salad

Dinner: Zucchini Noodles with Olive Oil

Snack: Homemade Fruit Bites

Drink: Oat Milk Vanilla Chai (no caffeine)

Broth: Fennel & Chamomile Digestive Broth

Day 21

Breakfast: Banana and Rice Pudding

Lunch: Silken Tofu Bowl with Rice

Dinner: Mashed Pumpkin Bowl

Snack: Soft Granola Cluster

Drink: Cooling Cucumber Smoothie

Broth: Miso-Ginger Broth

Day 22 to Day 28: Rebuilding & Energy Restoration

Day 22

Breakfast: Millet with Warm Pear

Lunch: Lentil Sweet Potato Patties

Dinner: Baked Rice and Pea Loaf

Snack: Soft Dried Mango

Drink: Ginger Banana Cooler

Broth: Simple Vegetable Mineral Broth

Day 23

Breakfast: Yogurt with Stewed Apples

Lunch: Baked Polenta and Carrot

Dinner: Broccoli Cream Pasta

Snack: Soft Rice Bars

Drink: Gentle Turmeric Tonic

Broth: Bone Broth with Carrot & Parsley

Day 24

Breakfast: Banana Pancakes

Lunch: Mashed Lentil Wrap

Dinner: Savory Sweet Potato Mash

Snack: Apple and Seed Butter

Drink: Strawberry Banana Smoothie

Broth: Ginger-Turmeric Healing Broth

Day 25

Breakfast: Rice Toast with Coconut Yogurt

Lunch: Steamed Veggie Bowl with Brown Rice

Dinner: Creamy Chickpea Pasta

Snack: Carrot and Hummus Scoop

Drink: Banana Oat Smoothie

Broth: Coconut-Lime Broth

Day 26

Breakfast: Warm Berry Compote with Oats

Lunch: Butternut Squash Puree with Rice

Dinner: Mashed Potato and Lentil Bowl

Snack: Cinnamon Apples

Drink: Lavender Honey Milk

Broth: Hydration Broth with Electrolytes

Day 27

Breakfast: Chia Banana Pudding

Lunch: Soft Chickpea Mash Wrap

Dinner: Baked Zucchini Rounds with Polenta

Snack: Applesauce and Granola

Drink: Vanilla Ginger Smoothie

Broth: Sweet Potato Comfort Broth

Day 28

Breakfast: Creamy Rice with Coconut and Apple

Lunch: Mashed Carrot Lentil Bowl

Dinner: Roasted Veggie Rice Bake

Snack: Banana Oat Muffins

Drink: Warm Herbal Milk

Broth: Mushroom Umami Broth

Conclusion

Nourishment Is a Language of Care

Burnout doesn't just drain the body—it unravels the self. At times like these, the world feels overwhelming—too noisy, too quick, demanding more than we can offer. But here, within these pages, is a gentler world. One where meals are not demands, but offerings. Where nutrition is not performance, but permission—to pause, to soften, to heal.

This cookbook was never just about food. It is about reclaiming the slow, tender rituals of self-support. Every broth simmered, every spoonful stirred, is a message: *you matter.* Even when you're shut down. Especially then. Because recovery from autistic burnout isn't linear—it's cyclical, sensory, sacred. And food, when tailored with intention, can become a balm for overstimulation, a stabilizer for dysregulation, and a bridge back to safety in your own skin.

Consider this your reminder: you are whole just as you are. You are burnt out. And rest, nourishment, hydration, and sensory respect are not luxuries—they are lifelines. You deserve them. Always.

So let your healing be full of softness. Let your meals be warm, repeatable, easy. Let them be enough.

Because *you* are enough.

Printed in Dunstable, United Kingdom

73177769R00071